ISBN 978-1-333-45702-0
PIBN 10506921

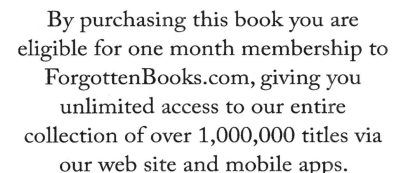

English
Français
Deutsche
Italiano
Español
Português

www.forgottenbooks.com

Mythology Photography **Fiction** Fishing Christianity **Art** Cooking Essays Buddhism Freemasonry Medicine **Biology** Music **Ancient Egypt** Evolution Carpentry Physics Dance Geology **Mathematics** Fitness Shakespeare **Folklore** Yoga Marketing **Confidence** Immortality Biographies Poetry **Psychology** Witchcraft Electronics Chemistry History **Law** Accounting **Philosophy** Anthropology Alchemy Drama Quantum Mechanics Atheism Sexual Health **Ancient History** **Entrepreneurship** Languages Sport Paleontology Needlework Islam **Metaphysics** Investment Archaeology Parenting Statistics Criminology **Motivational**

A

GENEALOGY

— OF THE —

CREHORE FAMILY,

— BY —

CHARLES FREDERIC CREHORE, M. D.

1887.

PRESS OF WARE & EATON.

WELLESLEY HILLS.

PREFATORY NOTE.

These imperfect memoranda of the family genealogy are published in the hope that those into whose possession they may fall will be induced to collect and transmit to the writer such information as may come in their way.

To facilitate making corrections it has been printed upon alternate pages, leaving the intermediate ones blank for the reception of notes.

It is not advisable to carry the records of descendants from FEMALE members farther than the third generation as they belong to the families whose name they bear, and this will be enough to enable them to connect themselves with their Crehore ancestry if desired.

All information sent to the undersigned will be carefully preserved in a special file for use in the future preparation of a more complete family history.

The writer has to acknowledge the welcome assistance of every member of the family whom he has addressed in relation to the work and especially to one whose complete memoranda regarding the earlier generations have much lightened his labors.

CHARLES FREDERIC CREHORE,

P. O. Box 1252 BOSTON. MASS.

NOTE.—Numbers in brackets upon left side of page, refer to immediate Ancestors. *Numbers in brackets* on the right of page designate the record of the person in the numerical order. The names of such are in capital letters.

THE CREHORE FAMILY.

Between 1640–1650 there appeared in Dorchester a young lad who went by the name of Teague Crehore. He was said to be of Irish origin, but as no such name occurs in the United Kingdom, it is probable that his surname was given an erroneous orthography ; all the more in that he could not, at a later date, write it. The Irish surname "Krehaw" corresponds phonetically with Crehore especially as the latter is pronounced by old residents of Milton and Dor. On the other hand many have thought it might be a mispelling of "Creagh". There is a tradition in the family that he had been abducted from his home and brought to this country when quite a child. The place of his birth and his true name must rest undetermined, probably, forever.

In regard to the date of his birth. An old Milton parish record gives his death as occurring June 3d. 1695, at the age of 55 years. As his widow took out Letters of Administration on his estate Jan. 22d. 1695, *Suffolk Probate rec. Lib. 10. fol. 723*, it is probable that the date of d. was Jan. instead of June. This would make his birth date about 1640. An old unrecorded deed formerly in the possession of Mr. Thomas Crehore, in which John Gill conveyed to T. a piece of Salt marsh, was dated Dec. 1660, at which time he was presumably of age. Among Suffolk Deeds Lib. 7, fol. 281, is the record of a conveyance by Teger and Mary Crehore to Robert Badcock of a piece of land bordering on the Neponset River, being the same bought by T. of John Smith of Dorchester, dated Jan. 21st. 1670.

He married, probably in 1665, Mary, said to be the daughter of Robert Spurr of Dorchester. There is no record of the marriage but her parentage seems to be generally admitted. Robert Spurr is mentioned in the Hist. of Dorchester, published by E. Clapp, Boston 1859, at pp. 232, 237, 279.

1. was buried in what is now the family lot in Milton Cemetery. There is no headstone and the exact spot is undetermined. Many of his descendants are buried about him. The Inventory of his estate extracted from the Probate record referred to above is as follows.

—INVENTORY.—

	£	s	.d
Wearing Apparell	5		
Dwelling house, Orchards & lands adjoyning	121	10	
Horse kind 4 £. Neat Cattle 17 £.	21		
Swine 2 £. Indian Corne 4 £ 10 s. Bailey & Rye 1 £ 10 s.	8		
An Acre of Salt marsh, said to be before by the deceased in his			
lifetime, verbally given to his son Timothy	8		
3 beds and furniture belonging to them	15		
Sheets, pillows, pillow bears and other linnen	2	18	
Sheep's wool 1.-1.-6. baggs 4 s. Spinning wheels 7 s.	1	12	6
Indian beanes 6 s. Saddle and panell old, 11 s.		17	
2 brass kettles, 2 brass pots and other brassware	2	2	6
Pewter 1.-14.-6. Earthenware 2 s.	1	16	6
2 iron pots, iron kettle and other ironware	2	2	6
Armes and ammunition and weights	3		
A table and 5 chairs	1		
Pails, trays, wooden tubs and seives		9	
5 barrells of Cyder 2 £ 5 empty barrells 10 s.	2	10	
1 Cart wheel, 2 p'r plow irons, 2 plow chains . . . . . . & iron bar	2	18	6
2 meat barrells and other small lumber		6	
In Money	4		
A debt due the Estate in money	3		
	£ 207	10s.	

Debts due from the Estate £14 13 s.

signed :

Tho's Vose.

George Sumner.

Eben'r Clapp.

Sworn to by Mary, administratrix, as all of the property of Teague dec'd.

For Teague's Children see next page.

NOTES AND MEMORANDA.

CHILDREN OF TEAGUE.

I.-TIMOTHY b. Oct. 18th. 1666. (2)

II.-ANNE b. Jan. 16th. 1668. ₁. Ebenezer Maxwell of Bristol.

III.-JOHN b. March 10th. 1669. (said to have d. early) unm.

IV.-ROBERT b. Sept. 29th. 1672. c. Nov. 4th.1696.

V.-IPSEBECK (?) b. March 19th. 1674.

VI.-REBECCA twin to above. m. Robert Pelton of Dorchester.

VII.-MARY b. July 31st. 1677. ₁. Henry Glover of Bristol.

VIII.-BENJAMIN b. July 22d. 1679. unm.

In Suffolk Deeds, Lib. 29, Fol. 186 is recorded a conveyance from Anne, Rebecca, Mary and Benjamin of all their interest in the estate of Tangue (Tauge?) Crehore &c. unto Timothy, eldest son of said deceased &c. This gives the names of the husbands of the daughters, specifies that those named were all of T's children then living, and shows that the mother, Mary, was alive at that date, Feb. 4th. 1714. Benjamin was unmarried at that date, as his wife, if he had one, would have joined in the release. He was then a resident of Roxbury. It is said that a Benjamin C. m. Rubamah ? at Roxbury and had son John b. April 1st. 1718, but all other accounts describe him as having never married. Mr. Jeruel Crehore had a mem. that "he disappeared and was never heard from." Of the daughters nothing more is known than appears above.

2.—TIMOTHY ² eldest son of Teague; b. in Milton October 18th., 1666. Yeoman.

In addition to his purchase of the homestead from his brother and sisters in 1714, *Suffolk Deeds, Lib. 29 Fol. 186,* he also bought a farm of 72 acres from John Vose, that adjoined the paternal estate, *Suffolk Deeds Lib. 33, fol. 159, also fol. 201, and Lib. 52, folios 21 & 175.* He m. Feb. 10th. 1688, Ruth Riol (Royal?) who d. June 27th. 1750. Both T. and his wife are buried in the family lot Milton Cemetery and their gravestones furnish authority for the dates given. D. Aug. 15th. 1739.

I.-TIMOTHY b. Dec. 1689. (3)

II.-RUTH. b. July 16th. 1692. c. Oct. 9th. 1724.

III.-JOHN b. Nov. 28th. 1694. (4)

IV.-SAMUEL b. Dec. 31st. 1696. d. unm.

V.-ISAIAH b. Jan. 7th. 1699. c. Nov. 3d. 1776 aged 77 y. unm., buried in Milton Cem. Said to have left his estate to John.

VI.-MARY b. May 6th. 1702.

VII.-HEPSIBAH b. Nov. 18th. 1705, d. Jan 21st. 1706.

VIII.-HANNAH b. April 29th. 1707, c. June 30th. 1707.

IX.-JEDIDIAH b. May 5th. 1710. unm.

X.-EBENEZER b. June 5th. 1713. unm.

NOTES AND MEMORANDA.

3.-TIMOTHY [3] b. in Milton Dec. 26th. 1689. Was a deacon in the Parish.

He probably lived on a portion of his father's property. Was a farrier by profession, m. Dec. 24th. 1712, Mary Triscoll of Dorchester. He d. Dec. 26th. 1755, in the 67th. year of his age. Buried in family lot.

> I.-HEPSIBAH b. Oct. 24th. 1713, d. in Dec'r Jan. 21st. 1805. unm. Had residence in Boston, Aug. 1771 as per unrecorded deed.
> II.-HANNAH b. July 11th. 1715, d. Jan. 11th. 1735 in 21st. year of her age. Stone in family lot Milton Cem. unm.
> III.-ELIZABETH b. July 23d. 1717. —
> IV.-RUTH b. Jan. 28th. 1719.
> V.-JEDIDIAH b. Oct. 19th. 1727. (5)
> VI.-WILLIAM b. Jan. 31st. 1730. (6)
>
> It seems probable that T. may have m. twice and that the last two were of the 2d. marriage. Possibly Mary Billings.

4.-JOHN [3] b. Nov. 28th. 1694 in Milton ; had the title of Captain. Lived on that portion of family estate lying at foot of Blue Hill. m. July 1st. 1724, by Rev. Peter Thatcher to Mrs. Mehitable Billings of Dorchester. (b. 1694. d. March 2d. 1787.) John d. Feb. 4th. 1759 aged 64 y. buried in family lot : grave marked by headstone.

> I.-MEHITABLE b. May 9th. 1725. m. Joseph Bent ?
> II.-MARY b. June 6th. 1728. d. Oct. 22d. 1748. bur. Milton Cem.
> III.-JOHN b. Nov. 8th. 1736. (7)

5.-JEDIDIAH [4] (Timothy [3] &c.) b. Oct. 9th. 1727. Lived in Milton on a portion of his father's farm. Two of three indentures, dividing the property between him, Hepsibah and William are yet in existence. They were not recorded. In them J. is described as a yeoman, H. as a Spinster, and W. as a Joyner. J. m. Chloe dau. of Gen. John Shepard of Stoughton ; ~~the date is not known~~. *3 ≐ 1754* She survived him and d. Aug. 25th. 1814, aged 81 years, buried in Wm. Crehore's tomb Mil. Cem. Jedidiah d. Sept. 28th. 1781. No record of burial.

> I.-TIMOTHY b. Aug. 21st. 175~~6~~ *4* (8)
> II.-HEPSEBETH b. Dec. 18th. 175~~6~~ *6* Was the 2d. wife of William Vose of Milton. Had Sukey Frances b. Mar. 7th. 1794. d. Nov. 22d. 1801, Reuben b. Feb. 19th. 1796. (m. Mar. 2d 1825 Sarah F. Hunting of Boston. Children Sarah Louise & John G.) d. in N. Y. Feb. 16th. 1877; and Sukey Catherine b. Jan. 17th. 1803, (. - Seaver, had 2 dau..) d. May 31st. 1832. H. d. Oct. 1843, aged 85 years.
> III.-SAMUEL b. Sept. 3d. 1761. (9)
> IV.-JOHN SHEPARD b. 1767. (10)
> V.-ELISHA b. 1771-2. (11)
> VI.-ELIZABETH b. 1780, m. Elisha Mackintosh of Dedham and died without issue in 1807, aged 27 yrs. L. Crehore has a mem. of her age as 32 yrs. making her birth in 1775.

NOTES AND MEMORANDA.

DESCENDANTS OF REUBEN VOSE. (5. II.)

I.–SARAH LOUISE b. Feb. 14th. 1827. 1. Nov. 5th. 1843, John VanVechten of New York. No children.

II.–JOHN GORHAM b. Mar. 18th. 1829, c. Mar. 17th. 1874. m. May 10th. 1855, Myra Raymond Haxtun (who d. July 15th. 1872,) and had: i. Flora Louise b. April 10th. 1859. ii. Raymond Hunting b. Aug. 1st. 1860. iii. Myra Haxtun b. July 31st. 1863. iv. Louise Van Vechten b. July 29th.1866, c. Aug. 25th. 1867. v. John G. b. Nov. 29th. 1867, d. Jan. 29th. 1868. vi. Louise Gorham b. May 21st. 1869.

DESCENDANTS OF SUSAN CATHERINE VOSE (5. II.)

Who m. CHARLES SEAVER at Boston, January 1st. 1824.

(NOTE.—The date of her d. (5. II.) should be corrected to read May 21st. in place of May 31st.)

I.–CATHERINE FRANCES b. Sept 20th. 1824. 1. Sept. 6th. 1853, Rev. Jacob R. Scott, has: i. Rev. Charles Seaver b. Feb. 15th. 1855, m. Sept. 27th. 1881. Jeannie I. Pond of Wrentham and has (Charles W. b. April 18th. 1883 and Roscoe Ellis b. Feb. 12th. 1887.) ii. Frank Richardson b. Sept. 13th.1857. 1. May 5th. 1880, Ida F. Rich of Chelsea, and had (Herbert R. b. Jan. 24th. 1881, Arthur E. b. Oct. 5th. 1882, c. Jan. 24th. 1883, Edith Frances b. June 22d. 1884 and Grace Belle b. May 21st. 1886.) iii. Anna Louise b. Aug. 8th. 1859, unm.

II.–MARIANNE PRATT b. Jan. 19th. 1830. m. Dec. 28th. 1848, Everson Leland of Holliston (who d. April 25th. 1885) and had: i. Annie Louise b. and d. Sept. 28th. 1849. ii. Charles Seaver b. June 21st. 1851, c. Oct. 7th. 1851. iii. Edward E. b. Oct. 19th. 1852. iv. Arthur S. b. June 22d. 1857. v. Frank b. June 22d. d. Sept. 30th. 1859. vi. Herbert M. b. Nov. 9th. 1865.

6.-WIIIIAM [4] (**3**) b. January 1st. 1730. Inherited one quarter of the paternal estate as shown in the indenture refeired to in (5) above. He m. Ann Bowen who d. Mar. 25th. 1797 aged 70 years. He died July 9th. 1803, buried in family lot in Milton Cemetery.

  I.-MARY b. July 16th. 1752.
  II.-WIIIIAM BOWEN b. July 6th. 1754.   (12)
  III.-HANNAH b. Sept. 26th. 1756. c. Oct. 16th. 1819.   unm.
  IV.-ABIGAIL b. Oct. 31st. 1758. c. Mar. 12th. 1812.   unm.
  V.-JOSEPH b. January 22d. 1763.   (13)
  VI.-EBENEZER b. Feb. 18th. 1764.   (14)
  VII.-BENJAMIN b.   1765.   (15)
  VIII.-FANNY b.   1767. c. Jan. 24th. 1824. aged 57 years. unm.
  IX.-THOMAS b.   1769.   (16)

7.-JOHN [4] (**4**) b. Nov. 8th. 1736. Was a Deacon in the Parish. Iived on a portion of the original property inherited by his father. m. Sarah Davenport (b. 1744. d. Dec. 27th. 1804.) He died Feb. 1st. 1805.

  I.-JOHN b. March 5th. 1763.   (17)
  II.-SARAH b. Feb. 17t1. 1774.

8.-TIMOTHY [5] (**5**) b. in Milton Aug. 21st. 1754. m., about 1780, Mary Sprague (who d. in 1805 aged 46 years.) He removed to Ashburnham Mass. where he d. Nov. 1st. 1843.

  I.-JEDIDIAH b. 1781. c. at Rochester N. Y. Dec. 13t1, 1856.
  II.-TIMOTHY b. April 1784.   (18)
  III.-MARY b. Nov. 4th. 1786. m. Nov. 1814 Asa Carpentei of Walpole N. H. and removed to Otisco Ononcaga Co. N. Y. d. in Rochester N. Y. Maici 2d. 1865. Children i. Tucy Mriiai Sprague b. Aug. 27th. 1815. 1. Ebenezer Gayloic. Is a widow living in Chicago Ill., 1as one child Oscai Eugene. ii. Asa Warren 1. Rachel Grinnell, 1as son Geo. Warren. iii. Mary Elvira b. Jan. 24th. 1819, m. Ec. Iuce of Haicwick Mass. Jan. 7th. 1841. Removed to Rochester N. Y. w1ere s1e now resices. Children: Ec. Rosson c. 1876. Acelaice m. Wm. H. Tupper. Minnie E. unm. and Clifforc A., lives in Rochester. iv. Marcia Alice d. young. v. Cyril Davis 1. fiist Clara Acais 1ac 2 children, and seconc Iouise Sawyer, one child.
  IV.-JOHN b. 1792. c. June 28th. 1829.   unm.
  V.-LABAN SPRAGUE b. Nov. 28th. 1794.   (19)
  VI.-WARREN b. 1802. c. Aug. 8t1. 1805.

9.-SAMUEI [5] (**5**) b. in Milton Sept. 23d. 1761. m. Jan. 19, 1785 Susanna dau. of Ezia Badlam (d. Jan. 31st, 1804 aged 38 years.) He d. Mar. 31st. 1807.
  I.-SAMUEL b. Sept. 5th. 1786. c. July 11th. 1788.
  II.-SAMUEL b. April 12th. 1789. Aitist. d. at Rio Janiero 1810. unm.
  III.-EDWARD b. May 9th. 1791. c. Dec. 12th. same yeai.
  IV.-EDWARD b. Nov. 19t1. 1793.   (20)
  V.-SUSANNA b. June 24th. 1796. c. in N. Y. city, w1ere s1e livec foi fifty years wit1 1ei cousin Reuben Vose, Feb. 23d. 1877.   unm.
  VI.-EZRA BADLAM b. Feb. 18th. 1799. Probably ciec in infancy.

NOTES AND MEMORANDA.

10.-JOHN SHEPARD [5] **(5)** b. in Milton 1761. m. in Dorchester Sept 9th. 1790, Hannah, dau. of ~~Elnathan~~ Iyon of Stoughton. (b. Apr. 5th. 1765. d. at Dedham May 7th. 1851.) Removed to Milton 1798 and to Dedham Sept. 1828 where he d. Jan. 7th. 1833.

 I.-LEMUEL b. in Dorciester March 2d. 1791.   **(21)**
 II.-CHARIES CRANE b. in Doi. Oct. 8th. 1793.   **(22)**
 III.-JEREMIAH b. in Dor. Dec. 19th. 1795.   **(23)**
 IV.-MARY SMITH b. in Milton June 1798. m. Oct. 10th. 1819, Josiua S. Bailey of Milton. Removed to Decia1 1826. c. Ap111 4th. 1832 Hac: i. Geo. Si1 1 ons b. July 29th. 1820. m. Jan. 4th. 1846, Eveline D. Dexter. c. Feb. 12t1. 1886. (Harriet E. b. Oct. 10th. 1846 and Georgiana F. b. Jan. 13th. 1851.) ii. Mary Elizabeth b. 1822. c. Nov. 14th. 1852. unm. iii. Iycia Ann b. 1825. 1. Jan. 21st. 1849 John P. Lynch. c. Ap1. 8t1. 1852. (Ella Gertrude b. Nov. 21st. 1849 and Mary Ida b. Mar. 10th. 1852.)
 V.-ELIZABETH b. June 7th. 1802. m. Dec. 2d. 1824, Josep1 Whiting of Decia1. (b. Dec. 31 1801. c. June 8 1861.) d. Jan. 3d. 1862. i. Ciailotte b. Jan. 25th. 1826. m. Henry S1it1 of Decia1 Oct. 29th. 1845. (Has 1ac fou1 children of w1o1 only t1e elcest survives. Josep1 Henry. b. Nov. 4th. 1847. m. June 5th. 1878, Frances Parry anc 1as Et1el b. June 24th. 1879.)
 VI.-HARRIET R. b. in Milton Mar. 16t1. 1806. m. Oct. 1st. 1828 Hezekia1 W1iting of Decia1 anc c. wit1out issue Mar. 19th. 1877. H. W1iting b. 1804. c. May 31st. 1876.

11.-ELISHA [5] **(5)** b. Dec. 11th. 1770. m. March 6th. 1791, Sarah youngest dau. of Henry Stone of Canton. (b. Oct. 6th. 1770. d. Sept. 4th. 1849.) Iived in Dedham where he d. May 4th. 1829.

 I.-DANIEL b. Nov. 21st. 1792. c. Nov. 16th. 1795.
 II.-ELISHA b. Aug. 15t1. 1794.   **(24)**
 III.-CLARISSA b. Mar. 24th. 1796. d. Sept. 13t1. 1800.
 IV.-SARAH STONE b. April 21st. 1798. m. May 8t1. 1818 to Fiancis Alcen of Deciam. d. Sept. 6th. 1866. Cuilcien: i. E1ily b. Sept. 12th. 1819. c. Mar. 12th. 1865. ii. Abne1 b. Jan. 29th. 1821. iii. Clai1ssa. b. Dec. 18th. 1823. iv. Maria b. Nov. 22d. 1825. v. Fiancis b. Ap1il 1st. 1827. vi. Hen1y C. b. July 1st. 1830. vii. Saia1 J. b. Mar. 14th. 1833. d. Dec. 31st. 1861. viii. Aceline b. Mar. 6t1. 1836. ix. Elis1a C. b. Sept. 25th. 1843. x. A1asa. b. Jan. 16th. 1849.
 V.-JOHN b. April 17th. 1800. d. May 8th. 1800.
 VI.-CLARISSA b. Jan. 18th. 1802. m. Jan. 7th. 1830, John D. Colbu1n of West Roxbury, c. Mar. 29th. 1876. Cuilcien: i. Ciailes Dexter b. Sept. 25th. 1830. c. Jan. 18th. 1842. ii. Saia1 Elizabet1 b. Ap1il 21st. 1832. iii. Elis1a Crehore b. June 11th. 1833. iv. Daniel Stone b. Aug. 15th. 1834. v. Lycia Davenpo1t b. Oct. 31st. 1836. vi. Jo1n Ly1an b. May 5th. 1838. d. Jan. 11th. 1857. vii. Hen1y Francis b. Nov. 24th. 1840.
 VII.-DANIEL S1ONE b. May 26th. 1806.   **(25)**
 VIII.-LYDIA DAVENPO1T b. Dec. 29th. 1806. m. Jan. 2d. 1831, Ciailes Fa1lington of Decia1. c. Ma1c1 9th. 1869. Cuilcien: i. Ciailes Hen1y b. Oct. 18th. 1831. c. April 27th. 1882. ii. Annie Rebecca b. Dec. 5th. 1834. c. July 11th. 1857. iii. Ecwa1c Crehore b. May 27th. 1837. c. Aug. 7th. 1865.

NOTES AND MEMORANDA.

12.-WILLIAM BOWEN [5] (**6**) b. July 6th. 1754 in Milton. d. May 13th. 1813. m. 1st., Lydia Billings (who d. Dec. 6th. 1785 aged 26 years) and had :

    I.-WILLIAM b. April 28th. 1781.   (**26**)
    II.-BOWEN b. March 29th. 1783.   (**27**)
    III.-LEMUEL b. Nov. 8th. 1785. c.   1810.   unm.

M. 2d., Rebecca Gulliver (who d. Nov. 5th. 1854 age 89 years, buried in W. Crehore's tomb M. cem.) They had :

    IV.-LYDIA b. Dec. 14th. 1794. m. Joseph Tucker of Milton, who afterward removed to Milford N. H. They had nine children as follows:
    i. George b. July 14th. 1812, c. Oct. 25th. 1867. m. Harriet A. Yeager. (One dau. Mary Ann b. Sept. 1851, c. Aug. 18th. 1860.) ii. Eliza b. Apr. 9th. 1815, c. June 7th. 1874. m. Nov. 15th. 1836, Porroy Rossitter. (One son, Charles P. b. Jan. 5th. 1848.) iii. William b. Aug. 2d 1817. m. 1st., H. E. Ruggles. (Two sons, Wm. Henry b. Feb. 23d. 1840 and Herman A. b. Nov. 23d. 1843, d. Jan. 21st. 1862.) m. 2d., Mary I. Boothby. (One son, Charles E. b. May 6th. 1847.) m. 3d., Eveline A. Tower. iv. Ann Rebecca b. Sept. 16th. 1820. m. May 27th. 1847, Charles H. Campbell. (Two children, Geo. H. b. Sept. 22d. 1850 and Annie L. b. April 27th. 1853, c. July 29th. 1856.) v. Charles J. b. Dec. 21st. 1822, c. Aug. 1st. 1852. m. Martha Wood June 25th. 1849, no issue. vi. Mary Lydia b. April 4th. 1825, unm. vii. Hannah A. b. Dec. 12th. 1827, c. April 4th. 1832. viii. James Crehore b. Oct. 26th. 1831, m. Nov. 16th. 1858, Maria Adelaide Sampson, no issue. ix. John Crehore b. June 3d. 1834. m. Jan. 25th. 1863, Mary Ann Adams. (Four children, Annie L. b. Mar. 14th. 1865, Nellie M. b. Nov. 30th. 1866, Jennie A. b. Oct. 25th. 1868, c. May 7th. 1882 and Joseph A. b. Dec. 5th. 1876, c. May 31st. 1882.)

    V.-JAMES b. Sep. 25th. 1797.   (**28**)

    VI.-REBECCA b. Feb. 23d. 1799, c. Jan. 26th. 1861. m. 1822, Tutter Paul of Newton, and had four children as follows:
    i. Sarah Rebecca b. May 25th. 1823. m. Jan. 2d. 1845, Arasa Crafts of Newton. (Three children, William Bowen b. Jan. 2d. 1847, Sarah E. b. Sept. 20th. 1851, Geo. H. b. Feb. 5th. 1853.) ii. Henry b. Aug. 3d. 1826. m. 1st., Mary A. Ward. (Five children, 3 c. infants. John Ward b. Dec. 15th. 1862, Charles Crehore b. Feb. 8th. 1866.) m. 2d., Mary E. Crippian. (Mary Rebecca b. Aug. 20th. 1876.) iii. Tutter b. June 16th. 1829. m. 1st., Mrs. M. E. Fish, no issue. m. 2d., Ellen D. Briggs. (Four children, Florence H. b. Jan. 5th. 1870, Tutter Gordon b. July 29th. 1871. Harriet O. b. Nov. 22d. 1874 and Irving C. b. June 29th. 1876.) iv. Harriet b. Oct. 30th. 1834. unm. v. Mary b. Jan. 15th. 1837. m. Sept. 11th. 1867, Marshall O. Rice. (Two children, Helen Rebecca b. Feb. 26th. 1869 and Wm. Henry b. May 14th. 1874.)

    VII.-JOHN b. Oct. 21st. 1806, c. at New Orleans 1833, unm.

NOTES AND MEMORANDA.

1785.

13.-JOSEPH [5] (6) b. Jan. 22d. 1763, d. Jan. 23d. 1813. m. Catherine Shuttle-
worth (b. Dec. 23d. 1763, d. Aug. 19th. 1851.) lived in Roxbury op-
posite to old Punch Bowl Tavern and had :

    I.-CATY C. b. Nov. 10th. 1787, d. Jan. 13th. 1867.   unm.
    II.-LEWIS b. Jan. 3d. 1792, c. July 4th. 1859.   unm.
    III.-HENRY b. Oct. 12th. 1793.   (29)
    IV.-ELIZA b. July 24th. 1798, c. Aug. 20th. 1817.   unm.
    V.-MINOT b. Nov. 3d. 1802.   (30)
    VI.-JULIA b. Sept. 20th. 1807, d. Jan. 27th. 1828.   unm.

14.-EBENEZER [5] (6) b. Feb. 18th. 1764, d. Sept. 23d. 1819. m. Hannah
Davenport (b. May 9th. 1764, d. Oct. 5th. 1835.) lived at Walpole, N.
H. Had :

    I.-HANNAH b. Aug. 1st. 1794. m. Aug. 1st. 1821, Samuel Johnson of Mal-
    den, had : i. Laura Crehore who m. Geo. F. Mann of Sharon and c. Nov.
    25th. 1886 age 64 years and 4 months. ii. Samuel.
    II.-CHARLES b. April 6th. 1797.   (31)
    III.-GEORGE b. April 12th. 1802.   (32)

15.-BENJAMIN [5] (6) b. 1765, d. Oct. 14th. 1832. m. Nancy Mellus (who d.
May 3d. 1854, age 79 years.) Lived in Milton, had :

    I.-ANN b. ?   unm.
    II.-BENJAMIN.   (33)
    III.-ZEBIAH ROYALL b. Feb. 29th. 1801, c. 1882.   unm.
    IV.-WILLIAM.   (34)

16.- THOMAS [5] (6) b.   1769, d. Dec. 31st. 1846. m. Eunice, dau. of
Silas and Lydia Houghton (who d. Dec. 31st. 1830.) Lived in Milton, had :

    I.-THOMAS b. Mar. 3d. 1793, c. July 25th. 1810.   unm.
    II.-EUNICE b. Feb. 27th. 1795, c. Jan. 6th. 1862. m. Aug. 1818 to Ben Vin-
    cent and had : i. Mary Aceline who m.   Weston and c. Dec. 1st.
    1869. ii. Thomas Crehore b. ?   c. Mar. 16th. 1825.
    III.-ISAAC NEWTON b. Nov. 21st. 1796, c. Oct. 31st. 1872.   unm.
    IV.-BEN FRANKLIN b. Dec. 3d. 1798, c. May 28th. 1828.   unm.
    V.-EDWARD b. April 13th. 1800.   (35)
    VI.-ADELINE BERRY b. Sept. 12th. 1802, d. Dec. 18th. 1843. m. Jan. 19th.
    1832, John H Rice of Boston, had : i. Mary Minot b. Nov. 19th. 1832, c.
    Mar. 8th. 1839. ii. John Henry b. Sept. 30th. 1834. m. Elizabeth A.
    Moise of Leominster (5 children, John F. b. June 10th. 1860, Mary A. b.
    June 12th. 1862, Minnie R. b. July 15th, d. Sept. 16th. 1863, Helen G. b.
    Aug. 2d. 1869 and Edith A. b. June 23d. 1877.) iii. Thomas Crehore b.
    Dec. 17th. 1836. m. Angeline S. Colburn of Welch, Me., no issue. iv.
    Elizabeth A. b. Mar. 29th. 1837. v. Franklin Crehore b. Oct. 2d. 1841. m.
    Nov. 23d 1869, Margaret Pierce of Coesse, Ind., has children.

    VII.-MARY ANN b. April 3d. 1804, c. May 16th. 1881. m. May 29th. 1834,
    Charles Hood of Taunton (b. Feb. 21st. 1787, c. Mar. 10th. 1864.) They
    had : i. Ellen Augusta b. Oct. 3d. 1836. ii. Charles b. July 27th. 1838.
    m. June 30th. 1880, Elizabeth R. Martyn of St. John, N. B. (had Mary
    Ellen b. Oct. 10th. 1881, d. Sept. 25th. 1882.) iii. Mary Caroline b. Oct.
    4th. 1840, c. April 27th. 1844. iv. Emma Tancon b. Feb. 18th. 1843. v.
    Thomas Crehore b. Mar. 27th. 1845, c. May 3d. 1851.

    VIII.-ELEANOR b. Mar. 22d. 1807, d. Oct. 25th. 1810.
    IX.-ELIZA b. Aug. 31st. 1808, c. Sept. 19th. 1816.

NOTES AND MEMORANDA.

17.-JOHN [5] (**7**) b. March 5th. 1793, d. Dec.   1819. m. Diana Ames and had:

    I.-JOHN AMES b. Jan. 25th. 1818.   (**33**)

SIXTH GENERATION.

18.-TIMOTHY [6] (**8**) b. in Ashburnham April 1784, d. Jan. 5th. 1866. m. Sally
W. Fairbanks (who d. Jan. 8th. 1869, age 75 years 5 months.)   They had:

    I.-WARREN b. 1803.   (**37**)
    II.-LEWIS b. 1807, c. Sept. 22d. 1850.   unm.
    III.-SALLY E. b. Feb. 2d. 1810, c. Mar. 18th. 1887. m. Oct. 21. 1833, Europe
      H. Fairbanks of Fitchburg.   They had four children of whom one
      survives: Albert J. b. Sept. 11th. 1849. m. Dec. 5th. 1869, Callie A. Knapp
      of Ashburnham and had Alice Isabel b. Oct. 16th. 1870, c. June 8th. 1879.
    IV.-HORACE b. 1812.   (**38**)
    V.-AUSTIN b. 1822, c Mar. 17th. 1870.   unm.
    VI.-MARY b. 1826. m. April 6th. 1847. Howard Marble of Jaffrey, N. H. and
      had: i. Eliza A. b. Nov. 18th. 1849, d. Dec. 15th. 1849. ii. Edward D.
      b. Feb. 13th. 1851. iii. Herbert E. b. July 13th. 1854, c. Oct. 19th. 1855.
      iv. Willie H. b. Feb. 8th. 1860, c. Nov. 10th. 1861. v. Charlie H. b. Sept.
      11th. 1863, c. Oct. 12th. 1865. vi. Frank A. b. Aug. 17th. 1868.

19.-LABAN SPRAGUE [6] (**8**) b. in Ashburnham Nov. 28th. 1794, d. Otisco,
N. Y. Oct. 9th. 1877. m. Oct. 31st. 1816, Marcia, dau. of fair Cone (b. in
Springfield, N. Y., Sept. 30th. 1797, d. Mar. 8th. 1844.)   They had:

    I.- LABAN MILTON b. Sept. 20th. 1817.   (**39**)
    II.-MARINDA b. Aug. 14th. 1820. m. Simeon O. Cooper who c. 1879, widow;
      no issue.
    III.-ASA CARPENTER b. May 5th. 1823.   (**40**)
    IV.-MARY JANE b. Dec. 17th. 1825, c. Aug. 22d. 1841.   unm.
    V.-MARCIA b. Aug. 14th. 1828. m. Aug. 16th. 1846, Clark C. Abbott, had:
      i. Alvah D. b. Aug. 19th. 1852. ii. Accie M. b. Jan. 31st. 1855. 1. 1st.,
      W. Barich, 2d. Richard Harris.
    VI.-SARAH ELVIRAH b. June 24th. 1831, c. Dec. 3d. 1848.   unm.
    VII.-ANSON JEDIDIAH b. Jan. 11th. 1834.   (**41**)
    VIII.-DELOS b. Sept. 26th. 1836.   (**42**)
    XI.-SYLVIA E. b. Feb. 7th. 1839, c. July 27th. 1882. m. Aug. 1863, Capt.
      Nathaniel A. Wright. 124th. N. Y. S. Vols, no issue.

20.-EDWARD [6] (**9**) b. in Milton Nov. 19th. 1793, d. in New Orleans 1833. m.
in N. O. and had son and daughter, the latter said to have m. there.

21.-LEMUEL [6] (**10**) b. in Dorchester March 2d. 1791, d. in Boston Aug. 18th.
1868.   1. Aug. 1st. 1827 Mary Ann Dodge, widow, daughter of Thomas
and Lydia (Farmer) Clark of England, (b. in England, Mar. 12th. 1795,
d. in Newton Jan. 1st. 1875.)   Lived in Newton and had:

    I.-CHARLES FREDERIC b. June 18th. 1828.   (**43**)
    II.-GEORGE CLARENDON b. Aug. 24th. 1832.   (**44**)

NOTES AND MEMORANDA.

22.-CHARLES CRANE [6] **(10)** b. Oct. 8th. 1793, d. in Boston, Feb. 12th. 1879. m. Oct. 1st. 1826, Chloe B., daughter of David and Katy (Bemis) Hartwell, (b. in Canton, Oct. 18th. 1805.) They had:

MARIA b. in Milton. May 29th. 1829, c. in Boston Nov. 12th. 1877. m. Sept. 17th. 1863. Gustavus Hay, M. D. and had Gustavus b. May 1st. 1866.

23.-JEREMIAH [6] **(10)** b. Dec. 19th. 1795 in Dorchester, d. in Dedham May 23d. 1876. m. Sept. 28th. 1828, Joann, daughter of Samuel and Sarah (Davenport) Dunbar of Charlton. Lived in Milton on homestead till 1844 and then removed to Dedham. Had:

    I.-MARTHA b. Aug. 5th. 1829, c. Feb. 17th. 1832.
    II.-ELLEN HAROD b. July 1st. 1835.   unm 1887.
    III.-AUGUSTA b. Jan. 7th. 1838.   unm 1887.

24.-ELISHA [6] **(11)** b. Aug. 15th. 1794, d. July 30th. 1841. m. Oct. 27th. 1822. Mary Watson Stearns of Waltham (b. Sept. 13th. 1797) where he resided. Had:

    I.-MARY WATSON b. Aug. 22d. 1823. m. June 5th. 1845. Samuel B. Whitney and had: i. Elisia Crehore b. Mar. 12th. 1846, lost at sea May 1866. ii. Mary Watson b. Sept. 11th. 1847. iii. Annie Maria b. Oct. 25th. 1849. c. Mar. 28th. 1852. iv. Acaline Stearns b. Jan. 17th. 1852. v. Charles A. b. Aug. 15th. 1855. m. Nov. 23d. 1881. Leila Nichols Porter (2 children, Elise Crehore b. Mar. 5th. 1883 and Thomas Lawrence b. Oct. 13th. 1885.) vi. Thomas Lawrence b. July 30th. 1857, d. June 26th. 1873.
    II.-MARIA STEARNS b. Mar. 17th. 1825, c. Feb. 23d. 1851. m. Dec. 10th. 1846. Leonard P. Smith and had: i. Ann Augusta b. Dec. 16th. 1847, c. Sept. 2d. 1850. ii. Mary Maria b. Jan. 1850, c. Nov. 14th. 1852.
    III.-ELISHA STEARNS b. May 26th. 1826.   **(45)**

25.-DANIEL STONE [6] **(11)** b. May 26th. 1804, d. June 22d. 1841. m. Mary Hart. They lived in Dedham, left no issue.

26.-WILLIAM [6] **(12)** b. April 28th. 1781, d. July 7th. 1864. m. Mar. 28th. 1810, Sarah Weld Clark of Claremont, N. H. (b. Aug. 24th. 1787, d. Nov. 21st. 1856.) Lived in Boston.

    I.-WILLIAM LEMUEL b. Feb. 1st. 1811, c. at New Orleans Sept. 7th. 1837. unm.
    II.-LYDIA BILLINGS b. Dec. 16th. 1812, c. Aug. 10th. 1883. m. Dec. 30th. 1840, Abraham A. Call of Boston. No issue.
    III.-THOMAS CLARK b. Aug. 21st. 1814.   **(46)**
    IV.-EDWARD VAN RENSELAER b. Aug. 28th. 1816, c. Mar. 27th. 1842. unm.
    V.-GEORGE AUGUSTUS b. Jan. 4th. 1819.   **(47)**
    VI.-SARAH WELD CLARK b. May 8th. 1821, c. Sept. 19th. 1822.
    VII.-LUTHER CLARK b. Jan. 26th. 1823, c. July 29th. 1846.   unm.
    VIII.-INFANT b. Feb. 10th. 1826, lived one day.

NOTES AND MEMORANDA.

27.-BOWEN [6] **(12)** b. in Milton Mar. 29th. 1783, d. in Boston July 27th. 1824. m. Dec. 20th. 1807, Hannah Tucker of Dorchester. They had:

    I.-HANNAH b. at Concord, N. H., July 29th. 1809, c. Aug. 30th. 1829, unm.

    II.-WILLIAM BOWEN b. at Concord, N. H., Feb. 25th. 1811, d. at Mobile, Sept. 14th. 1839.   unm.

    III.-CLARISSA b. at Concord Jan. 23d. 1813. m. at Boston May 27th. 1831, Ansel Lothrop.

    IV.-ANN b. at Dunbarton, N. H., June 16th. 1815. m. July 30th. 1844, Samuel H. Root of Boston and has: i. Sarah Burbank b. Sept. 10th. 1845. ii. Oliver Bowen b. Mar. 19th. 1848. iii. William Crebore b. Dec. 18th. 1851. iv. Samuel Henry b. Aug. 16th. 1854.

    V.-SARAH b. at Medford, Mar. 20th. 1820, c. at Castleton, Vt., Jan. 19th. 1849.   unm.

28.-JAMES [6] **(12)** b. Sept. 25th. 1797, d. April 12th. 1880. m. in 1832, Mary Ann Abrams. Lived in   Left no issue.

29.-HENRY [6] **(13)** b. in Roxbury Oct. 12th. 1793, d. May 24th. 1879. m. 1st., May 7th. 1820, Susan, dau. of William and Polly Simonds Larbell (b. 1794, d. Feb. 13th. 1832.) They lived in Malden, Mass. and had:

    I.-HENRY b. Jan. 8th. 1821.   **(48)**

    II.-SUSAN b. Sept. 22d. 1822, c. May 10th 1883. m. Sept. 18th. 1851, James Cox of Malden.

    III.-JOSEPH b. Aug. 11th. 1824.   **(49)**

    IV.-JULIA AUGUSTA b. Dec. 13th. 1828. m. Nov. 30th. 1851, Judge Austin D. son of Nathan and Lucy Knight. Reside in Hallowell, no issue.

Married 2nd., April 4th. 1833, Hannah, dau. of James and Susanna (Newhall) Hitchings b. Jan. 10th. 1808, d. Oct. 2d. 1866 and had:

    V.-JOHN MURRAY b. Mar. 30th. 1837.   **(50)**

    VI.-CATHERINE SHUTTLEWORTH b. Aug. 6th. 1838. m. Nov 1865, George W. son of Edward and Eliza L. Bell (d. Jan. 1882) and had: i. Grace Clifford b. 1866, d. 1880. ii. Florence b. 1873.

    VII.-JAMES MINOT b. 1841. d. Nov. 18th. 1849.

    VIII.-GEORGE HITCHINGS b. 1842, d. Nov. 22d. 1849.

    IX.-HANNAH HITCHINGS b.   1844. m. June 9th. 1870, Charles Henry, son of August and Johanna Burchman of Saxony (b. July 21st. 1842) lives in Brooklyn, N. Y. No issue.

30.-MINOT [6] **(13)** b. Nov. 3d. 1802, d. Oct. 22d. 1858. m. July 24th. 1836, Lydia, dau. of Hezekiah and Eunice Rogers French. Lived in Lincolnville, Me. from 1832. Left no issue.

31.-CHARLES [6] **(14)** b. at Walpole, N. H. April 6th. 1797, d. Oct. 21st. 1831. m. Feb. 8th. 1826, Lucy Bowker (d. 1876.) Lived in Walpole and had:

    I.-JOHN DAVENPORT b Nov. 22d. 1826.   **(51)**

    II.-GEORGE b. Dec. 18th. 1827.   **(52)**

    III.-ELEANOR b. Feb. 20th. 1830, d. in Cleveland, O., Dec. 2d. 1883. unm.

    IV.-CHARLES b. Dec. 25th. 1831.   unm.

NOTES AND MEMORANDA.

32.-GEORGE [6] **(14)** b. April 12th. 1802, d. July 8th. 1882. m. Jan. 1st. 1827, Clarinda Harvey (b. Dec. 8th. 1801.) lived in Chicopee, Mass. and had :

    I.-CLARINDA b. Aug. 24th. 1828, c. Aug. 31st. 1847.   unm.
    II.-HARRIET b. Feb. 3d. 1831. m. June 9th. 1853, Atwood D. Holbrook of Charlestown.
    III.-GEORGE B. b. June 16th. 1832.   **(53)**
    IV.-ROSE A. b. Dec. 24th. 1833.   unm.
    V.-LOUIS D. b. May 23d. 1835.   **(54)**
    VI.-ASAHEL b. Feb. 18th. 1837, d. Sept. 28th. 1863.   unm.
    VII.-MARY JANE b. Aug. 21st. 1839, c. Nov. 15th. 1859.   unm.
    VIII.-CHARLES EBENEZER b. Nov. 3d. 1841.   **(55)**

33.-BENJAMIN [6] **(15)** has descendants living but no record has been furnished.

34.-WILLIAM [6] **(15)** The only record I have is d. Aug. 24th. 1858. m. Eliza (d. Nov. 16th. 1871.)

35.-EDWARD [6] **(16)** b. at Mattapan April 13th. 1800, d. April 27th. 1867. lived in Dorchester and Boston. m. 1st., Sept. 4th. 1822, Mary Preston (b. Oct. 5th. 1802, d Mar. 15th. 1838) and had :

    I.-THOMAS b. Mar. 15th. 1823.   **(56)**
    II.-EUNICE ELIZABETH b. at Dorchester Sept. 2d. 1825, c. Mar. 22d. 1873. m. April 2d. 1846, Horatio Harris of Boston (b. Feb. 12th. 1821, c. Feb. 29th. 1876) and had : i. Horatio b. Feb. 26th. 1847, c. Feb. 13th. 1871. ii. Edward Crehore b. June 29th. 1849. m. June 8th. 1870, Florence E. Howe of Roxbury and had : (Florence M. b. Nov. 29th. 1871, d. Sept. 14th. 1885 and Paul F. b. Dec. 15th. 1872, d. Sept. 25th. 1885.) iii. Minnie b. Aug. 21st. 1854. m. Feb. 10th. 1880, Joseph, son of Phineas Stone of Charlestown and had (Harris b. Dec. 1880, c. Aug. 12th. 1881 and Marian b. Oct. 14th. 1882.) iv. Georgia Anna b. June 27th. 1860. m. Mar. 31st. 1887, Fred W. Kennedy, M. D. of Lawrence.
    III.-MARY b. Oct. 3d. 1827, m. Oct. 9th. 1849, Thomas Edward Moseley of Boston (b. Nov. 5th. 1823.) They have : i. Edward Crehore b. Aug. 21st. 1850. m. Oct. 17th. 1872, Ellen Slace Wheeler (b. May 10th. 1853) and had : (Mary b. Nov. 21st. 1873 and Edward C. b. April 21st. 1875, c. Mar. 1st. 1876.) ii. Frank b. Mar. 30th. 1854, m. April 29th. 1880, Martha Alger, dau. of Charles Hawes (b. Aug. 1858) and have : (Elise b. July 1883.) iii. Arthur b. April 19th. 1861, c. Feb. 29th. 1864. iv. Horatio Harris b. Dec. 15th. 1866, d. Nov. 12th. 1869.
    IV.-BENJAMIN FRANKLIN b. May 23d. 1830.   **(57)**

He m. 2d., July 20th. 1843, Sarah Minns Tileston of Dorchester, b. July 16th. 1810,) and had :

    V.-EDWARD b and c. Aug. 14th. 1844.
    VI.-EDITH b. Oct. 28th. 1846.

36.-JOHN AMES [6] **(17)** b. Oct. 25th. 1818, d. Jan. 21st. 1877. m. June 3d. 1839, Sarah Bass. lived in Milton on the family place, but d. in Medford. He left no issue and the line of descent through John [3] closed with him.

NOTES AND MEMORANDA.

SEVENTH GENERAIION.

37.-WARREN [7] (18) b. 1803, d. Mar. 20th. 1882. m. Mar. 1st. 1831, Saiah Be is of Winchendon (d. Sept. 26th. 1864, age 56 yeais.) They had five children whose na es and birth dates are not ascertained by the compiler.

38.- HORACE [7] (18) b. 1812, d. Jan. 6th. 1881. m. June 12th. 1844, Mary Bowkei of Phillipston. They left no issue.

39 - IABAN MIITON [7] (19) b. Otisco, N. Y., Sept. 20th. 1817, d. Oct. 1883. m. 1st., Dec. 1845, Maria Knight by whom he had no issue. m. 2d., Oct. 15th. 1865 at Charlotte, Mich., Emily Foidham (widow) and had:

    I.–JOHN M. b. at Brookfield, Mich., Sept. 20th. 1866.

40.- ASA CARPENTER [7] (19) b. at Tully, N. Y.. May 5th. 1823. m. 1st., Elizabeth Ann Crowell (d. Oct. 7th. 1873.) Iives in Michigan and has:

    I.–MARCIA I. who m. Claience Foidham (son of Eiily who m. Iaban M. and ias: i. Kittie A. b. Nov. 23d. 1876. ii. Clyde A. b. Feb. 22d. 1881 iii. Mina A. b. April, 1886.
    II.–ISAAC WILIIS b. Mar. 12t1. 1859. i. Jan. 19th. 1887 at Minneapolis, Mo., Maigaiet C. Kennecy.
    III.–CLARENCE WRIGHI b. Mar. 26th. 1864.

He i. again and has two children, but I have no precise iecord.

41.-ANSON JEDIDIAH [7] (19) b. Otisco, Jan. 11th. 1834. m. Jane F. Karle and has:

    I.–EDWARD KARIE b. Feb. 15t1. 1872.
    II.–FRAN K MIITON b. Dec. 23d. 1879.

42.- DEIOS [7] (19) b. Otisco, N. Y., Sept. 26th. 1836. m. Mary Jane Gieen and has:

    I.–WILLIAM D. b. May 16th. 1866.

43.- CHARIES FREDERIC, M. D. [7] (21) b. in Newton June 18th. 1828. m. Sept. 29th. 1857, Maiy Wyer, dau. of Henry and Elizabeth Faıris (Iracy) Ioiing of Boston.

    I.–FREDERIC MORION b. at Newton July 16th. 1858.
    II.–ELIZABETH TIACY b. at Boston Dec. 21st. 1859.

NOTES AND MEMORANDA.

44.-GEORGE CIARENDON [7] **(21)** b. at Newton Aug. 24th. 1832, d. at Boston Dec. 23d. 1870. m. Nov. 7th. 1855, Iucy Cathaiine, dau. of Otis and Maiy Ann (Grout) Daniell of Boston. They had:

    I.–MARY ANN b. at Boston Feb. 28th. 1857. m. Oct. 16th. 1879, Stanley Cunningiai of Boston,' ias: i. Stanley b. Nov. 20th. 1880. ii. Geoige Claiencon b. Oct. 25th. 1882. iii. Maiy b. Apiil 12th. 1885.

    II.–MORTON STIMSON b. at Newton Sept. 21st. 1858. m. at Cohasset Sept. 6th. 1883, Alicia Viiginia, dau. of Heniy Wateis Robson anc Maigaiet Ellenor (Joinson) Stewait, anc iac: i. Infant son b. Oct. 15th, 1886 c. Oct. 17ti. 1886.

    III.–CATHAiINE IEIGHTON b. at Newton Feb. 14th. 1862. i. Sept. 4th. 1884, Robeit Aioiy. M. D. of Boston, ias Robeit b. Oct. 23d. 1885.

    IV.–CHARLES IEMUEI b. at Boston, Feb. 6th. 1867.

    V.–LUCY CLAiENDON b. at Boston Aug. 5th. 1871.

45.-EIISHA SIEARNS [7] **(24)** b. at Waltham May 26th. 1826, d. Nov. 2d. 1852. i. June 13th. 1850, Martha Manson, and had:
    I.–ELISHA b. 1851, d. Jan. 7th. 1853.

46.-THOMAS CIARK [7] **(26)** b. Aug. 21st. 1814, d. Feb. 11th. 1873. m. Coidelia Dole, had:

    I.–CAROLINE m. Mr. Renous and ias ciilcien.

    II.–WIIIIAM I. no infoi iation obtainec.

    III.–LUTIIERA m. Mr. Goulc anc ias ciilcien.

47.-GEORGE AUGUSIUS [7] **(26)** b. Jan. 4th. 1819, d. Sept. 28th. 1875. m. Mar. 27th. 1842. He has no children. The naie of his wife has not been furnished to ie by my informant.

48.-HENRY [7] **(29)** b. at Malden Jan. 8th, 1821. m. in Iincolnville, Me. Dec. 28th. 1848, Maiy A., dau. of Isiael and Alice Studley (b. May 15th. 1820) have:
    I.–JULIA ELIZA b. Nov. 1st. 1849. c. Dec. 10th. 1879. m. Oct. 12th. 1876. Calvin W. Iayloi of Winslow, Me.

    II.–ALICE JANE b. Sept. 17th. 1851. m. Oct. 9th. 1874. Augustus A. Fletcher.

    III.–JOSEPH b. July 10th. 1853.

    IV.–MINOT b. Aug. 28th. 1855.

    V.–HARRY b. Sept. 22d. 1858.

    VI.–Infant b. June 16th. 1862. c. July 3d. 1862.

    VII.–FRANK ADAMS b. May 7th. 1864. c. May 30th. 1867.

49.-JOSEPH [7] **(29)** b. Aug. 11th. 1824. m. May 17th. 1854, Ellen Ieiont, dau. of Jaies W. I. and Julia Gilbeit Mitchell, (b. Ieeds, Me. Aug. 13th. 1824.) Cleigyian of Univ. Ciuich, now settled in Biockton (1887), has no childien.

NOTES AND MEMORANDA.

50.- JOHN MURRAY [7] **(29)** b. March 30th. 1837. m. 1st., Dec. 18th. 1860, Lorania B., dau. of David and Susan King of Whitefield, Me. (d. in California 1880.) left no issue. m. 2d., Feb. 8th. 1882, Annie, dau. of Alexander and Effie Cum ings. Resides in Charlestown.

51.- JOHN DAVENPORT [7] **(31)** b. in Walpole. N. H., Nov. 22d. 1826, d. in Cleveland, O. Oct. 7th. 1884. m. Dec. 30th. 1862, lucy Williams (b. Feb. 7th. 1841) was a Civil Engineer, residing in Cleveland, Ohio. Had:

    I.-WILLIAM W. b. Feb. 3d. 1864.
    II.-AIBER1 C. b. June 8th. 1868.
    III.-MARY I. b. Mar. 8th. 1870.

52.- GEORGE [7] **(31)** b. in Walpole, N. H., Dec. 18th. 1827. m. 1st. July 27th. 1857, lucy Ann Gage of lawrence, Mass. (d. Aug. 18th. 1875.) lived in Illinois and had:

    I.-GEORGE PHINEAS b. Sancoval, Marion Co., Feb. 23d. 1862.
    II.-MARY ALICE b. Betralto, Macison Co., Aug. 29th. 1864.
    III.-HELEN ELIZA b. Betralto, Macison Co., Dec. 23d. 1866.
    IV.-HATTIE lOUISA b. Sancoval, Marion Co., Mar. 19t1. 1869.
    V.-CHARLOTTE lUCY b. Sancoval, Marion Co., June 21st. 1871.
    VI.-JESSIE EDITH b. Sancoval, Marion Co., Feb. 15th. 1873, c. May 28th. 1876.

He m. 2d., Sept. 17th. 1876, Charlotte J. Whiston (Hoffman) of Chicago, by whom he had no issue. He removed to St. louis, Mo. in 1877 where he follows his profession of Civil Engineer, and m, 3d., Oct. 3d. 1883, Alice Middleton (Williams) Glover of P. E. I. and has no children by her at this date, 1887.

53.- GEORGE B. [7] **(32)** b. June 16th. 1832, d. July 22d. 1877. m. July 16th. 1857, Keziah Walker (d. Dec. 12th. 1883.) lived in Sheffield, loraine Co., O. and had:

    I.-CLARINDA C. b. May 1858., d. Sept. 16th. 1858.
    II.-GEORGE R. b. Jan. 22d. 1860. m. Sept. 20t1. 1882, Nellie E. Faragrer anc 1as: i. George J. b. June 25th. 1883. ii. Etna C. b. Sept. 16th. 1885.
    III.-GRACE E. b. July 7th. 1860, c. Jar. 11th. 1884. 1. Oct. 2d. 1883, Rev. l1os. W. DeLong, anc livec in Fredericksburgh, O.
    IV.-CHARLES J. b. Sept. 22d. 1872.
    V.-ROBBINS B. b. Oct. 18th. 1876.

54.- LOUIS D. [7] **(32)** b. May 23d. 1835, d. Oct. 29th. 1860. m. Dec. 2d 1868, Mrs. Minnie V. Holt left no issue.

33

NOTES AND MEMORANDA.

55. CHARIES EBENEZER [7] **(32)** b. Nov. 3d. 1841.   m. 1st. Nov. 30th. 1869, Edna F. Carter of Surry, N. H. (d. May 10th. 1879.)   Iived in Chicopee and had :

  I.–FRANK H. b. Sept. 5th. 1870.
  II.–CHARIES W. b. Mar. 19th. 1874.
  III.–BERIRAM D. b. Dec. 18th. 1877, c. Oct. 10th. 1878.

m. 2d., Oct. 18th. 188**1**, Olive I. Chapin and has :
  IV.–RALPH C. b. Nov. 10th. 1884.

56.-THOMAS [7] **(35)** b. in Dorchester March 15th. 1823, d. in Boston Jan. 16th. 1875.   He m. and had six children, viz : Belle, George, Cora, May, Frank and Anna.   Of these I only know that Anna m. J. A. Whitmore of Biunswick, Me. and has dau. Florence Stowell b. Oct. 6th. 1881.

57.- BEN. FRANKIIN [7] **(35)** b. May 23d. 1830. m. at Lunenburgh, Mass. July 17th. 1857, Sarah A., dau. of Ezra and Melissa Curtis (b. April 3d. 1838. d. at Medfield June 29th. 1885.)   Had :

  I.–FRANK EDWAɛD b. Groton May 10th. 1858, c. Ieominstei, Sept. 12th. 1859.
  II.–CARRIE AUGUSTA b. Clappville Nov. 20t1. 1862, c. Roxbury, Jan. 4th. 1865.
  III.–MARY ADELINE b. Clappville Mar. 6th. 1865. m. at Medfield Oct. 29th. 1884, Rev. J. Nelson Parcee, Unit. Ciurc1, t1en settlec at Iaconia, N. H,
  IV.–EDWARD b. Clappville Dec. 6th. 1866, d. June 4th. 1867,
  V.–FANNY MELISSA b. Clappville Aug. 18th. 1869.
  VI.–BEN. FRANCIIN b. Medford Sept. 21st. 1873.